Music in the Church

Kenneth Palmquist

Contents

Music in the Church

- Introduction
- The pattern – the prototype from heaven.
- Beauty and order in the music.
- Harmonic Series – the series of overtones.
- The development of the pattern among the first Christians.
- How should Christians respond to the music tradition
  by the first Christians?
- Wordless music and jubilations.
- The hymns (songs about and to Jesus - called Christ Hymns).
- The song with / in spirit.
- Some genres in polyphonic Western music.
- Conditions for how the glory of God can rest upon individuals
  and the Church in their music-making.

Practical exercises for the Church

- Exercise 1 To discover the possibilities of voices.
- Exercise 2 To discover how musical instruments work.
- Exercise 3 Working with melodies.
- Exercise 4 Working with musical notation.
- Exercise 5 Working with pulses and rhythms.
- Exercise 6 Working with timbre, accords or harmonies.
- Exercise 7 Working with performing practice.
- Exercise 8 Working with instrumentation.
- Exercise 9 Working with forms and structures.
- Exercise 10 Working with bodily expression.
- Exercise 11 Working with the listening culture in the Church.
- Appendix

Workbook for composers and musicians

- Introduction.
- Some basic reflections based on the order in the overtone series.
- Exercises.
- The pattern from David – a summary with Bible passages

Preface

When the people of Israel made a tent (tabernacle) for worship in the desert, the original was a heavenly reality. When God builds His Church, He does so from a heavenly prototype. In the Old Testament, he introduced different physical prototypes, which then received their interpretation in the New Testament. Two of these models were: the tabernacle in the wilderness and the Temple in Jerusalem. When it came to the music at these gathering places for the people of Israel, God showed His heavenly model of the tabernacle in the desert under Moses' leadership. During David's reign in the 1000's B.C., a music culture was founded around a new tabernacle (in the Old Testament, several names were used such as David's hut and the tent of meeting). The music of David's tabernacle followed a model that he had received from the Lord's hand. This model then formed the tradition in Israel until the Temple was destroyed 70 AD. How did the tradition develop then? What was the attitude of the early Christians to this pre-forming music?

In this book this subject will be discussed.

Ljungskile, Sweden April 2016

Kenneth Palmquist

Introduction

I have previous written a book about Music in the kingdom of God. See also **http://kennethpalmquist.hemsida24.se/**

This is a continuation about how the local Church can cooperate with God to restore the Levite service. The Levites had this ministry during the time of the tabernacle and also at the time of Moses and David. A tabernacle was a tent where the people of Israel gathered. It was the most important place for worship before the temple in Jerusalem was built. The service continues later in the temple of Solomon, Zerubbabel, and Herod the Great. In Psalm 81: 1-6 we read that praise was already a commandment from the Lord when the Israelites walked out of Egypt.

I have used New King James version in the Bible quotations.

1. The pattern – the picture of the heavenly reality

During the time of King David, the Levites followed a heavenly prototype, a **pattern** that David and the prophets had received from the Lord. It formed the basis of worship in Israel in 11th century BC. This pattern was one of the patterns that was fulfilled in Jesus Christ. The original was from God and was fulfilled in Jesus Christ. In his letter to the Ephesians, Paul wrote about a *plan* that would be implemented in Christ (Ef.1: 10). In Greek, the word for plan is *oikonomia*, which means management, administration and order. Jeremiah also told of an order in Jer. 31:36 (comp. Jer. 33:25). It is an order, a covenant with day and night, which carries the entire universe. This covenant upholds everything in the universe. This is, for example, about how the fundamental laws were originally created and are held together in the universe. The sounds of creation are working based on the fundamental laws in the universe. The sounds of creation are created and are held together by God's *oikonomia*; by God's command; by God's order in Christ. It is God, through Jesus Christ, who keeps creation together. It involves coordination in the kingdom of God, for which the pattern of David was one of the models. This pattern also includes God's orders for the music in Israel.

This order of the universe - summed up in Christ - was the basis for the theoretical laws and rules of which audible music in Israel was an outflow. In the Christian Church, music was subordinate to the order, the plan that was fulfilled in Christ Jesus. The universe is not chaos but has a very beautiful order that testifies to divine beauty, God's own being. Creation - the entire universe - can be described as God`s wonderful and beautiful symphony.

In the book Music in the Kingdom of God part one I have illustrated what this creation symphony and the music that was performed according to the pattern were, and are, all about. (See also a summary in points on the last page.)

I am now going to teach in more depth about how this pattern – this order for the music – emerged during the early Christian period and how it can be perceived and developed in the Church today.

David got – as far as I know – not theoretical laws for how the music would work, but rather instructions – *in writing by His hand,* which included *all the work of the service* in the temple– and was inspired by the Holy Spirit. (1 Chron. 28:11-19)

This pattern had an external form:

> 1. The Levites had a specific order for each day of the music. In the morning and evening the Levites would thank, praise and worship in connection with the sacrifices.
> 2. Sometimes they sang antiphonal.
> 3. A leader took up the song - often with the help of an instrument.
> 4. They had an apprenticeship system to train new Levites. It was an education in order to make them willing, skillful and to take responsibility.

The words in the songs of David found in the Psalms can be read in different languages and dialects, but there are no written musical notes in the Hebrew text, until the Masoretes wrote their "musical note". There are in fact no theoretical music laws or regulations in the entire Bible.

It seems that God looks at the different languages, sounds and language melody as things that do not need to be written down in exact rhythm and melody lines. Therefore, He did not restrict the pattern to a linguistic or language melodic model. In such cases, certainly God also gave the pattern precise musical content, which was scribed down. There is an oral tradition. However, this Israeli tradition was not sufficient to express the whole pattern. It was not enough for God with a beautiful Israeli tradition. The revelation of the Messiah would prove to be the heart of the pattern that God presented to David. The pattern was greater than a nation's outer traditions. The Christian Church is directed to the order; the plan that God has created, and that was summarized in Christ. The Church is referred to this order in Christ that is created by God, to the Holy Spirit's guidance, to the Bible's testimony, to Israelis oral traditions and also to the research.

In the book Music in the kingdom of God (p. 37-40) I have described the Israeli music traditions at their gathering places. The Church needs to understand that it has wandered far away from its origin, nearly cutting off its Jewish roots. To some extent, in order to understand this, we need to see how Jesus and the first apostles related to music in the temple. When God Himself came and camped (tabernacle) in Israel through Jesus (John 1:14), it was also a fulfillment of covenants, including the covenant with David. Through Jesus came the fulfillment of the Messianic Kingdom, which also includes the music.

Jesus and the early Christians challenged the temple service. Jesus described himself as the Temple and taught about another center for worship and adoration. It was in and through Jesus - the new temple - that the praise of God and the new song, would be established and would continue. Jesus said that the Father wants true worshipers who worship in spirit and truth. Jesus criticized all forms of superficial religiosity. The Levite service would be moved from Jerusalem to the heart of individuals - both Jews and non Jews i.e. Gentiles. These persons then formed the called out collective (Assembly, congregation, Church - *ekklesia*). The Church gathered together in various places (synagogues, The Stone Hall in Jerusalem, individual houses and later in buildings called Churches).

The first Christians continued to hear and read Tanach - the Old Testament. They also worshiped Jesus as Messiah and Lord. This worship lived in the hearts of the first Christians, but was also heard through the voices, mouths and other instruments. One of the evidences of audible song by the first Christians is found in the Book of Acts (chapter 16). Paul and Silas had been imprisoned, and at night they sang. All the prisoners in the prison in Philippi heard Paul and Silas singing. This also demonstrates that their praise was strong at this time. Paul and Silas were not ashamed to sing strongly. How did they sing? The Greek word for singing praise is *hymneo*. It means to sing a hymn, a song of praise to someone. Perhaps it was a so-called Christ Hymn - a hymn to Jesus Christ. We can consider how two strong male voices would have sounded in the prison vaults.

The audible part of singing by the first Christians followed the tradition of the Israeli people - the pattern from David - but with a deeper meaning. This deeper meaning was preached by Jesus and also by the first Jewish apostles. (It was about this deeper restoration of David's tabernacle.)

When Paul gave the Churches direction about audible music, in two of his letters, it was a clear continuation of the restoration of the pattern of David. Therefore, it is important to study David and the pattern to see how the psalms were used in the first Christian Churches.

In this booklet, I review how the Church can continue to work based upon this pattern. I do so in the conviction that there is no other foundation upon which to build the musical life in the Church. The research about the Israelis music continues. Both the Israelis and the Christian oral traditions, the interpretations of rabbis and Christian theologians can, of course, be questioned. But basically there is already so much research that we can speak with some general consensus.

This consensus among scientists and theologians, concerning the external form of this read-vocal musical tradition, is not primarily about details such as - precise language rhythms, language melodies, pitches, whole melodies, rhythms and timbres - but more about the forms in which this music emerged.

Carl-Allan Moberg summarizes these similarities in his musical history as follows: [1] (My comments in parentheses.)

- A reciting lectures on firmly restrained tones (This is about the monotone song reading.)
- Melodic figures as boundary markers in the hymn text structure, i.e., middle and end, often at the beginning of each verse. (These figures are small melody motifs at the beginning, middle and end of phrases in the psalm text.)
- A more developed melodic style that consists of combinations and variations of recurring motifs. (This was an improvised song starting from short motifs. These motifs were based on certain modes, i.e., scale, similar a key.)

In addition to this common structure, one can also find common modus (scales) and melody motifs. The Israeli foundation that rested on the pattern of David could show (according to Idelsohns research in the early 1900s) that the ancient oral traditions of the Israeli people had survived with admirable ability, particularly in the Diaspora and in remote areas in Yemen. So scientists are not without evidence, but interpretations differ slightly.

When the Romans had destroyed the temple in Jerusalem in 70 A. D. and the Jews had failed in their rebellion against them; the Jews survivors continue gradually to sing psalms and hymns as a sacrifice of praise to the Lord. Of course, there were many individuals who could remember the vocal tradition from the temple. The great research by Idelsohn about the different Jewish traditions in Diaspora.

---

[1] Musikens historia i västerlandet intill 1600 Natur och Kultur 1973 p. 51

(Thesuarus of Hebrew Oriental Melodies 10 band 1914 – 32 and Jewish Music 1929) is very important in relation to the Jewish history tradition.

But how far back can we find the connecting links to this documentation? In the deepest layers, you can follow the thread down to the Masoretic notation which was completed in the 10th century AD, but Idelsohn means that some layer extends at least as far as the first century. A D. (See the book Music in the Kingdom of God p. 43-46.) Talmud says that the Bible shall be read in public and made understandable for the listeners through a beautiful, musical melody. The Rabbis said that you get a deeper understanding of scripture by singing it. In Idelsohn's book "Jewish Music", one can also read about how he looked at the four tone modus (tetracord) that formed the basis for the motives. Behind the melodic motives, there was a whole theoretical school whose roots extend deep into history.

Synagogues have, like Christian communities, been affected by growing music epochs and development. This means that many different styles of music can be found in synagogues too. The Jews, like the Christian congregations, are divided in their opinion about this influence (ranging from the most orthodox to the most liberal.)

When Jesus comes back, it will be the *Lord's praise in Jerusalem,* which will be the starting point for the music in the nations. *The name of the LORD will be proclaimed in Zion and his praise in Jerusalem, when nations and kingdoms come together to serve the Lord* (Ps. 102: 21-22). This then becomes God's own restoration of the pattern of David. Until then, there will be a cultural diversity that the congregation has to relate to. Some Christians think that there ought to be great diversity of musical styles in the Church. I also believe that God wants this diversity and variety, but the question is what *kind* of diversity. Satan's kingdom has also diversity.

2. Beauty and order in the music

David urged Israel, and all other nations, to use their voices and instrumental resources. The Levites would use voices and instruments in a beautiful and holy way. *Play beautiful* says Psalm 33, and *Praise Him according to His excellent greatness* is settled in Psalm 150. This means that the Levites had a yardstick that was greater than themselves, when they composed and performed music. The Levites would know God, and then let themselves be influenced by the Holy Spirit in composing and performing. (Their own taste was not the basis for their conviction.) The relationship with God and the Holy Spirit's influence was the condition for the beauty and glory in the music. The consequence was that they used their voices and instruments in a way that was in harmony with God's own beauty and glory. In their relation to God and practical service, they used their voices and instruments in a natural way, based on the order of creation, which in turn was rooted in God's own being. In the heavenly head office, the fundamental order or plan (*oikonomian*) expressed through Jesus Christ, is the fulfillment of God's thoughts with his creation (Ephesians 1). This means that all music must be measured in relation to the beauty that shines in Christ. This order, this beauty can also shine from the Christians (2 Corinthians 3:18; 4: 5-6). **This is the foundation of the beauty and glory of the music in the Church.**

The awareness of beauty or intuitive sense of beauty that man received at birth is a gift from God. This gift can be both used and abused. There is, in man, an awareness of beauty that often manifests itself when he enjoys the order and beauty of God's creation. When man slips away from God and begins to worship the creature, his mind becomes darkened. (Rom 1.) Even if the external beauty of the music of the Church is rooted in the order found in the creation, the Church needs to understand that this order, or the laws, are grounded in Christ. The origin of the whole of creation is not a power, but a person expressed through Jesus Christ. In the deepest sense, it is upon him that music in the Church is based, not upon creation or human consciousness of beauty.

Man's awareness of beauty shows that he has the capacity – albeit limited - to find beauty in melodies, rhythms and harmonies. When the Spirit of God influenced the Levites, their awareness of beauty also grew. This meant that the Levites were subordinate to God's holiness and beauty. They did not roar bizarre sounds with their voices, or blurt out any discordant sounds from their instruments. (The people of Israel did so when they followed the Baals – their idols 1 King. 18:28-29). This does not mean that God can be hard of hearing or threatened by any violent sound that humans can make, but it does mean that humans have limitations, which are important to take into account. It also means that the possibilities that music sounds can give, also can become a form of idolatry in contrast to the pattern from heaven and the inner awareness of beauty and responsibility.

In the days of David, the Levites and the early Christians had primary responsibility before God concerning the order, form and beauty of music.

Godless people will naturally not give this great attention but a Christian should. Godless people often set up norms and standards for what they consider to be beautiful or good music. Personal taste or fashion trends will be the starting point.

However, the Levites obeyed God and allowed themselves to be inspired by him in lyrics, melodies, rhythms, harmonies, instrumentation and performance practices. (In Greek philosophy, musicians imitated their gods). So the main difference between the Israeli and Greek´s music was about where the inspiration came from. David, the prophets, and the Levites saw creation as a testimony of God. The psalms have a very positive view about creation, in spite of the power of sin and death. Then the Levites also acknowledged the beauty of the creation of single instrumental tone where the harmonic series, or so called series of overtones is the pattern. (See the book Music in the Kingdom of God p. 73-76.)

So, these following three pillars were clearly in Israel's music:

- The beauty, order, forms and sounds that God has created. All this was a demonstration of his mighty person. He is greater than his creation, but he is also immanent in his creation. All things in creation work through Christ. (Hebr.1)
- The beauty and construction (pattern) of a single tone was a natural starting point for play and research. This beauty was also an expression of God's being.
- The pattern that David received.

An Israeli lyricist and Levite musician had:

1. a generous opportunity to play, improvise, research, build, compose, and perform music. Neither Jesus nor the apostles renounced this generous attitude, which was founded in God's benevolence and mercy to the people of Israel. Every Levite in the temple stood in this God-given benevolence, while they were subordinated to the tradition that had been built up by skilled and trained Levit leaders. They were - when the music was at its best - subordinated to the custom that David and the prophets had set up. The music reflected the character of God. And they would hand over the pattern. Example of how the people of Israel would hand over messages, etc. is available in many places in the Bible. A clear example is the book of Joel 1: 3. Already in the time of Moses songs were handed over. Deuteronomy 31:22, 30. See also Ps 78:5-7 The praise of the Lord would be handed over from generation to generation. Ps 79:13. This oral part was not written down similar as the words were. It was at 3th century A D that this tradition began subscribed also in the "musical notes".

2. laws that warned them not to adapt to how nations around Israel played music. When Israel was right before God, God established the Levite service. It was both a music that was filled with God's generous good will towards His people, and a clear tradition with a clear holiness. They were separated for holy service.

The melodies, rhythms and harmonies that the Levites composed, or indeed the harmonies heard at the various places for worship, were thus composed based on the pattern received by David and the prophets from the Lord. This pattern comes from a relationship with the Lord. When the Levites were inspired by the Spirit of God their performance of melodies, rhythms and harmonies sounded beautiful measured from God's viewpoint. Then the music was a conformation or a figuration of an established heavenly pattern in sounding form, grounded in God's own way of composing in creation. This should also be the basic attitude of every Christian composer, musician and Church.

When we look at creation, it isn't based only on mathematical formulas and laws. In the Bible, the beauty of creation is also described in more poetic words. People generally don't describe a babbling brook in mathematical terms. They use totally different expressions.

The Psalms describes music in creation with deep respect for God and His beauty. Praise to the Lord, His glory and beauty sounds throughout all of creation. God has in the Psalms collected His music in a concentrated form with the help of people in the Old Testament time. This music behind the ink of the written words is varied just as in creation, but also impregnated of **order, beauty, unity and rest.** The music of the early Church had the same basic principles.

In his first letter to the Corinthians, Paul wrote about the external order and clarity of music. He meant that there was a connection between clarity in the music and the order and clarity in spoken words. (1 Cor. 14: 7-12). For Christian composers and musicians it means that music must be in order and have clarity. It is never a question of chaos and harshness in the Church of God. **Order, peace and beauty are the cornerstones of creation. These must also be the foundational stones reflected in music by the Church.**

3. Harmonic Series – the series of overtones

In David's time, the Levites probably played music out from different scales based on the harmonic series. (They had overtones in the silver trumpets. Harps were stringed and tuned in some form of keynotes, from which scales could be formed. Flutes were capable of over-blowing, and some form of common tones - when they had holes.) Harmonic series is a gift from God and can be seen as **God's musical alphabet.** Other musical alphabets should be seen as human constructions that can be used, but not defended as something universal. The different tuning of instruments, as for example the equal tempered scale is not something universal. The acoustic oscillations in the harmonic series, forming the so-called just intonation is however the tuning that God has given a single ton of creation.

Se also: https://en.wikipedia.org/wiki/Harmonic_series_(music)
https://en.wikipedia.org/wiki/Musical_tuning

The white key on a piano, which represents tones, was formed in the improvisation and exploration based on the harmonic series. This is quite an international way to build tone material of different pitches, even if they are not divine or universal. When God created melodies, he was not confined to any particular harmonic series. Birds sing melodies with very different kinds of tone steps. (Most birds don't follow a special series of tones. God has composed the majority of birdsong based on sound, not on the basis a single harmonic series)

There are so called scales in the overtone series. The natural oscillation that form so-called steps in the overtone series is the scales in the overtone series. In the creation different tones are mixed together to different types of cluster. As with the basic sounds (phonemes) in the human voice, so are ordinary tones an opportunity to find different music languages/styles and musical dialects. (There are thousands of music languages / styles and dialects.)

Some of the musical instruments of the Israeli people were probably made based on the harmonic series pattern. The instruments in the Bible can be divided into families:

- blowing family
- string family
- percussion family

These families have historically been divided into other families such as family woodwind, brass, keyboard and strings. David had at least 20 different instruments.

4. The development of the pattern among the first Christians

When Jesus and the disciples sang psalms (Matthew 26:30), it was a natural part of the Jewish Passover. They were not Levites, from the tribe of Levi, but they sang psalms. It was also natural for the first Jewish Christians to continue to sing the psalms.

We know that the first Jewish Christians in Jerusalem gathered in Solomon's Colonnade (in Judaism called Stone Hall) to worship the Lord. This place was a kind of open-air synagogue where many Jews were gathered together - a place similar with the Western Wall. It was a crowded place for reading – to recite the Tanach, discuss biblical texts and to pray. This was also a well-attended place where the Levite musicians could teach songs from the Temple. It is said that there was a contemporary Levite musician called Joshua ben Hananya who served in the Herod temple in the first century. After his service in the temple, he went to the Stone Hall, together with other Levites, in order to lead the daily worship there. (Werner: The

Sacred Bridge page 24-25) The Stone Hall was also a place where *maamadots* were collected. They had a kind of intermediate position between the synagogue and the temple, an important link between the chosen clergy and laymen in the synagogue. In that way, the temple songs could be handed over by more persons than the Levit priesthood. So the atmosphere in the Stone Hall was a murmur of voices, like in the Western Wall today with songs from the Psalms, among other things.

Maybe there were Jewish Christians who had learned the psalms by the Levites or through these *maamadots.* There are no written note documents showing the musical links from these first Christian oral traditions to the first recorded psalms with noted accents. But there are descriptions of the form around the melodies. Christians read or recited texts in their services. It is also told that "someone" sang songs between the text readings. From early sources, we can read how "someone" sang one of the Psalms of David and the rest of the congregation responded by imitating or just singing the last words of the verses. Probably this "somebody" knew the psalm tradition from the temple. From this singing, between "somebody" and the Church, grew a kind of refrain (antiphon) that the Church later sang.

Clemens I- a leader in Rome in the first century A.D. - wrote a letter to the Corinthians in which he urged the Church to continue to pray the threefold Holy. (Hebr. *kedusha*), which was an established and important part of the worship in the temple and in the synagogues. In a similar way, the first Christians continued to sing the Psalms and they composed new hymns and prophetic songs under the influence of the Spirit. In this way any Christian can sing and pray the psalms and go deeper and deeper into praise and worship until they through the Holy Spirit become translucent with the glory from God.
Tertullian, a Christian leader, reported in the third-century A.D. how the Christians sang, either from the Scriptures or newly composed songs. (Tertullian: Apology 39)

All this shows the links between the Jewish songs and the form in which Jewish Christians continued to recite and sing.

But how did it sound? To delve deeper into this subject, it is necessary to read the research books by Idelsohns and Werner. Werner shows that the musical notes which grew out The The Masoretes work - which was given its final form by Aaron ben Asher of c 850. A.D. - provide the basis for the music that had been passed down to generation after generation through the tradition bearers (through Jewish hazans -

singer). Was this first Jewish musical notation a record of the pattern from David? We do not know, but what we do know is that rigorous regulations and faithful tradition bearers have surrounded the Jews scriptural and oral traditions. Early on, there was leading the singers with the hand and fingers (cheironomi). Therefore, we can assume that there are deep connections between the Masoretic signs, the first Christians singing and deeper down to the pattern by David.

The Bible talks a lot about conveying God's teachings from generation to generation. Jesus and the apostles affirmed, of course, the true doctrine and tradition, but they were against bad habits, false teaching and false tradition. The continuation of the pattern among the first Christians was both **audible** and had the **same forms** as the Jewish pattern. The pattern was fulfilled in Christ and was formed and heard among the first Christians as a deeper fulfillment of the restoration of the tabernacle of David. The forms and the melodies were probably not exactly the same as when the pattern at David's tabernacle began or among the Levites in the temple of Solomon, but the main characteristics and forms were probably the same. So, the external form was similar to the pattern, but the inner life and glory had been moved from the physical temple in Jerusalem to the Christian Church. That doesn't mean that God had abandoned the Jewish people or the land Israel, but it meant that the Gentiles would be a part of the covenant with David and the established house of prayer - the tabernacle of David.

The Glory (*shikina*) - God's own personal presence - that was the most important in the temple, dwelled, according to John (John 1:14), in Jesus. In his prayer before the Passion, Jesus also said that he had given glory to his disciples. (John 17:22) So the most important part of the pattern was this shekina - glory. God's presence was in both Jesus and his disciples. This was also the inner beauty in the worship among the first Christians. The audible beauty of music was important, but the glory of God in individual Christians in the Church and through the music was and is the most important. The first Christians lived in Christ, who was and is the glory from God and looked at music as an outflow of the relationship they had with the living, resurrected Christ. Their relationship with Jesus Christ and their relationship with each other in the Church were the most important building blocks (Rom15.5-13). So the audible music of the first Christians rested safely on the Old Testament teaching and also upon continued renewal among both Christian Jews and Gentiles.

More links in the tradition chain

If we seek after the links between psalm singing in the Temple of Jerusalem and the growing Christian community until the 4th century, we need also to ensure that:

- Paul spoke much about the tradition that he handed over to the Churches in Asia Minor. The Swedish researcher Birger Gerhardsson describes this very clearly in his paper about the prehistory of the Gospels (Nova Press). In this tradition, they read, chanted and sang from the Scriptures of which the psalms were a natural part.

- The tradition after Paul shows that the Church was exhorted to hold firmly onto the **"fast rules for service"** (Clemens I letter to the Corinthians). This meant that they would hold onto the teaching by the Apostles and reading of the Old Testament, which also included the service of praise and worship. (Acts 2:42; 13:2) The Christians had this service both individually and together when they gathered. Moreover, it appears that they also held onto the basic order of the synagogue at their meetings. Paul's letter shows that, particular in the letters to the Corinthian Church. (See the book Music in the Kingdom of God p. 204-208 .)

- This tradition is clearly documented in the generations after the first Christians. The first Christians and the following generations, up to the 4th century, founded the tradition of memorizing and reciting the Scriptures (OT) and Jesus' teachings. (1 Timothy 4:13)

- From the 4th century until the 7[th]century, this psalm tradition developed to different traditions, which were gradually written down like the Masoretic notation.

- The differences between the psalm traditions among the Christian Churches have been explored and will continue to be explored.

5. How should Christians respond to the music tradition by the first Christians

As I have written in the book, reading aloud, recitation and cantillation have been a part of the construction of the Israeli music and the first Christians worship. There is no reason for an individual Christian or Church to minimize this. Therefore I would like to encourage Christians to read texts aloud, both individually and together. I would also encourage individuals, and churches, to chant songs that have been cantillated through the ages. Of course, recitations and cantillations - like all forms of music - can also be an art or tradition that celebrates itself, where hearts aren't involved.

In about 1450, some of the Protestants in Geneva became convinced that psalm singing from trained choirs in the Roman Catholic Church had no place in the Church or individual Christian life. This, I believe, was an overhasty conclusion. Luther disagreed with Calvin and the Reformed (see common Church history). The psalms had been sung namely since the early Christian period (although not with trained choirs in the beginning, but by "someone" and by the congregation as a whole). There is no doubt that, during the first 1500 years, much of the Roman Catholic Church had gone through an apostasy with false doctrines and meaningless traditions. Despite this, not all adoration and worship in the entire Christian Church, and that by Christian individuals was corrupt.

But the motive for singing hymns after the principle of reciting texts is not, however, founded in the Orthodox or Catholic Churches hymn traditions. The motive rest in the pattern of David, and, therefore, in God's own plan with music.

The different psalm traditions in synagogues around the world and in historic Churches are simply variations on recited and cantillated psalms. Of course, some psalm traditions cannot claim to have historical roots and to be connecting links to the first Christians.
Is it important to find and hold on to this tradition? Yes! For the first Christians this tradition was important - even in the non-Jewish communities. This should motivate

all Christians and all Churches to seek out this deep root. It does not mean, however, that all traditions of Churches were healthy and proper during the first two centuries.

Some psalm traditions in Christian history are very melismatic, many notes on one syllable. This has sometimes been challenged on the basis that the congregation did not get a good understanding of the text and that the texts are too much decorated. This problem has been discussed throughout history. In fact, it is about to what extent the Church wants to allow wordless music in the Church.

6. Wordless music and jubilations

Wordless music and so-called jubilations have occurred throughout Biblical history. The Bible clearly encourages nonverbal music. The nonverbal music has, of course, among other things, been used to beautify and decorate, besides being a tool for exultation and adoration. The Church may, therefore, express its nonverbal joy, its joy to God for His creation, His word and His mighty deeds. Of course, the danger is that the Church may be more interested in learning and performing nonverbal music than hearing the words of the Bible and sermons. Augustine warned against the idolatry of the beauty of music and the feelings that it creates. The warning was justified, but maybe not perceptive enough. God has clearly preached in the whole of creation with wordless music (sound). Therefore, I believe it is important that the Church also preach, praise and play joyfully with the possibilities of wordless music. But, **how** is the big question! Sing, shout with joy and play beautifully attune with God's beauty is what the Bible tells us.

The hymns (songs about and to Jesus - called Christ Hymns)

The history of the Christian hymn can be followed from the first Christians' praise to the only known written hymn with notes from Oxyrhynchos in Egypt in 2nd century. The various branches can then be followed through history. (See hymnology.)

The hymns that the Church chooses and the way they are performed are a sort of sowing and reaping. The Church is exhorted to sow and reap in the field of the Holy Spirit. This means that the content of the hymn text must be true and reflect Jesus Christ in all musical garments, as well as in the performance.

The song with / in spirit

This song is also possible to trace through history. (See the book Music in the kingdom of God p.81-82.) The wordless jubilation before the Lord has often broken out where the Spirit of God has worked. The opinion that the song with the spirit died after the first Christian generation has no historical ground. Therefore, the Church ought to be open to the guidance of the Holy Spirit in this part of music in the Church. Paul's teaching is the foundation and guidance.

7. Some genres in polyphonic Western music

Notation in the Christian Church was first developed in the 9th century. Monophonic unison singing was probably the dominant music in large parts of the Christian Church until the 9th century. From 9th century onwards, you can follow the Western development of polyphony. During 11th century, the line system for notation was developed and polyphony became more possible (Guido of Arezzo). There had been polyphony before, but in the 11th century it developed further. For a long time, unison singing with the unison and octave intervals was seen as the perfect consonances. With polyphony, the fifths and the fourths were accepted as consonances. In England there was also the third, an accepted consonance.

Generation after generation began to examine the various intervals in the overtone series.

Polyphony can - as it developed in the Christian Churches throughout Europe – be seen as a continuation of decorations on biblical texts. In Music in the kingdom of God p.163-164, I describe how, through theoretical rules, the Church tried to keep these decorations in a modest way.

Historically, there has clearly been two different ways to build polyphony:

- Several melodies are built on each other and form polyphony (so-called horizontal thinking).
- Polyphonic sounds (chords) have been formed on the basis of composing melodies
  (so-called vertical thinking).

When melodies began to be added, different harmonies appeared. Some intervals were more accepted than others. This formed the pattern for different music theory systems, based on some kind of philosophy. The development of Musica Enchiriadis (the first known noted polyphonic music) through the epochs Ars Antique, Ars Nova and to the full acceptance of major and minor harmonies as consonances was naturally based on the overtone series (see common music history). When they began to examine consonances and dissonances (discordant intervals), it was thus based on personal philosophy and personal taste. This greatly affected the development of music.

The polyphonic development of the West was thus a consequence of the overtone series, but, at the same time, it was founded and valued upon the basis of subjective human examination.

It was during the Ars Antiqua period in the mid 11th century that the first known contrapuntal rules began to appear. (It's about rules for which intervals, rhythms and harmonies could be used in the polyphony and how they would be used.).

Two clear rules became prominent:

- "In the beginning of the first bar it should in all modi be consonance without regard to whether the first is a longa, brevis or semibrevis." (This rule meant in practice that you would choose consonances on accentuated bars. Exceptions were made for the syncope.)
- the third, and the sixth began gradually to be used as full consonance. The fifths combined with the octave in the stressed parts were during the Ars antique period still the most dominant.

During the Ars Nova period (1300-1450), major and minor triads became more prominent and later during the Renaissance (1450-1600) they completely dominated. During the baroque period (1600-1750), composers built on major and minor thinking with a freer dissonance treatment. The dissonances sevenths and nona became more and more accepted as consonances, but settled after some music theory rules. Between 1600-1750, Baroque music developed in Europe. During the Age of Enlightenment, new ideals developed. They wanted "simpler", more "transparent" music but, at the same time, they wanted to express more emotion in it (Haydn, Mozart, Beethoven). The chromatic scale became a symbol of how one could use the new dissonances in a new way. This led to the Romantic period where tonality dissolved more and more (R Wagner). (J Brahms and others continued to stubbornly hold on to tonality.) The so called atonality developed and research and experimentation with the sound continued.

Creation is full of timbres (clangs). It thunders, rumbles, rustles, howls and roars. During the 20th century, when composers researched and experimented with sound as starting point, it opened endless possibilities. Of course, God is not astonished when he hears and sees all human research and experimentation with sound, but he subdues music from the ungodly (Isa. 25: 5). He simply puts a dampener on the wicked music, and the end will be God's judgment of the music machinery in the whole of Babylon. (Rev. 18: 21-23.) This does not mean that God limits human freedom to play, improvise, research, compose and make music. It means that God, besides subduing music from the ungodly, has set a limit upon how far human beings can and may destroy themselves and others using sound.

The question is which spirit and philosophy are governing the composition and performance of the music. From the Church's perspective, it is important to know which spirit, philosophy, and thinking are leading composition and performance.

Music, which is based on a different fundament other than a respect for God and his beauty, always leads to distorted pictures, perverse art and destructive sound.

There are some composers in the 21th century who continue to write music based on consonance and dissonance thinking. Several composers are finding their way by composing sounds that correspond to either their own or other people's taste of beauty.

As a Christian, I mean that there is no better foundation for philosophy and performance of music than that found in the Bible. Consequently, it is important that order, form and beauty are formed. Chaos, formlessness and random music cannot, therefore, be accepted in the Church. However, the Church ought always to talk about the relationship between consonant and dissonant sounds. In this talk, there are two trenches:

- Too detailed personal taste perceptions.
- Too "high ceiling" where no restrictions may be accepted.

Throughout history, Christians have been building up different theoretical music systems. They have improvised, researched and discussed how melodies, rhythms and harmonies should be designed. During their time, some people broke out from the thinking and habits that were prevalent. This resulted in various styles and musical dialects. If you want to learn the handicraft in these styles, you often need to learn the rules that formed these styles. (If you, for example, wants to learn Renaissance style in Europe in the 16th century one needs to study the rules for the music at the time, to be able to compose in the same style.)

The Reformed, Puritan and Pietism Church branches reaction against the Catholic Church and the Lutheran Church for the artistic trappings, was understandable although, in my opinion, not the right way to go for Christianity. Despite much good that has come out of the Reformed and pietistic traditions, their thinking is not convincing in the subject of music in the Church. They did not build their thinking on a sustainable biblical position. Often it has been personal taste and strong oppositions to the established Church, which have influenced their opinion. Therefore, the Reformed and Pietistic Churches formed their own traditions.

I mean that the Church was and is called to be the head and not the tail, even in the subject of music. There have been examples in Church history where Christian musicians with their music have influenced more than their own generation. In addition, they made music that also spoke to some people outside the Church. They showed that it is possible for Christian composers and musicians to give a credible witness of a restored music culture.

Personally, I am convinced that it is possible for the Church of God to receive composers and musicians and guide them into a deep relationship with the Lord. I am also convinced that the Church has the responsibility to bring them into a deep understanding of the importance of unity in the Church. When this happens, the glory of God will come upon composers, musicians and the Church.

8. Conditions for how the glory of God can rest upon individuals and the Church in their music-making

The Levites were dressed in white linen. In the light of the new covenant, it is about the righteousness that comes by faith through Jesus Christ. This righteousness is one of the basic fundamental pillars for the glory of God to rest upon a man and a Church.

In 2 Chron. 5:13, it was also about **coordination** and **unity**. In the NT, it was about unity in Spirit and coordination of practical thinking. It was also about coherence (one accord. See the book Music in the kingdom of God p. 83-87.) The Hebrew word *kol echad* means one sound. This shows the coherence among the musicians. I have given an interpretation in the book Music in the kingdom of God (p 85). Chapter 15 in the letter to the Church in Rome is an important passage to understand unity and coherence. Paul discusses unity in the Spirit and conformity in practical issues. This was and is the fundamental ground for the Shekinah – God's glory, which came over musicians and the Church.)

When the Lord seeks beauty in music, he seeks these cornerstones (righteousness, coordination, unity and coherence). The Lord gives unity if he receives a people who are willing to follow him. The glory of the Lord is the best thing a composer, musician and Church can get. The glory of the Lord is synonymous with his presence in a specific time and space. The glory of the Lord is more important than all musical beauty and perfection. Therefore, the conditions for His presence are more important than what man can create through musical perfection and expression. Man (it applies to all people) can create neither the righteousness of the saints, nor unity and coherence. These are gifts from God through faith in Jesus Christ.

Neither puritan rules and simplicity, nor musical abundance, beauty and perfection can in themselves create the glory of God.

The external beauty of music is a matter of respect and reverence for God and his word. When a composer has this reverence for God, he has the basic foundation in his composition. But when righteousness, truth and unity are established, there is even greater potential for the outer audible music to become beautiful.

Practical exercises for the Church

What will then the practical consequence of following Jesus be in the field of music when we have the pattern from David as compass?

First the Church need to understand that the oral tradition, as the people of Israel had was more complex before it was noted than after. The Church therefore needs in addition to praying and studying the Bible also to research, analyze and by extension have a strategy in the form of a well thought-out theory of music, based on the music's material, form and handicraft. This is essential if the Church wants to cultivate an external audible musical tradition that is in harmony with the new song - which broke out through Jesus - and also in harmony with the tradition that Jesus and the apostles handed over. We also need to be conscious of how we perform. It is a seed that bears fruit.

Musical craftsmanship has the same potential as other arts. In addition to teaching about music's origins and function, the Church needs to practice songs and learn what it means to use music as a tool to serve God.
The Church needs to get an understanding of how musical craftsmanship functions; how music is constructed; used and the effect that it can have. Therefore, the Church needs to study music to some extent.

I give a few practical suggestions as to how the Church can establish and hold on to this musical tradition. It is important the Church understands that worship in spirit and truth is a service to God. This is, together with sound teaching and good morality, among the most important principles in the Church. (John. 4; Eph 5: 19-20). The Church needs to have a healthy attitude to Bible teaching, moral lifestyle and worship tradition, where the teaching, thanksgiving, praise and worship with tones, rhythms and sounds was, and ought to be, a natural part. In this present time, it is also to do with what kind of music individuals, families and Churches are listening to and choosing to cultivate.

The practical exercises that I present here are basically for the whole Church. Not all the exercises are for the whole Church and the workbook that follows this teaching is more for composers and musicians and those who might be leading music in the Church.

I also recommend a book by Fabian Staahle: *Awake, awake sing your song*. This book is about how every individual believer can worship Jesus with their own songs, without the need of any formal musical education. It can be ordered from Lulu.com

Exercise 1
To discover the possibilities of voices

It is necessary that the Church teach about God's view on the human voice.

The first sounds that a fetus experiences is probably the mother's voice. It is important that the Church has a positive attitude to the human voice. The voice is a gift from God. Early on, children should be told that they have **beautiful** and **strong** voices, created by God. The voice will be used throughout life. It is a very delicate instrument. The voice needs, therefore, to be nurtured and trained to work well. This positive view of the human voice needs to be sowed into children early on.

The first exercise is therefore about discovering the possibilities of the voice.

1. Discover different **blowing sounds** through throat, tongue and lips. (Don't use the vocal chords.)

2. Discover also whistle sounds.

3. Discover blowing sounds through the hands as instruments.

4. The **vocal cords** can be practiced in many ways. In the appendix 1, I give some suggestions of exercises.

5. Practice vocal chords by the consonants b, d, g, j, l, m, n, r, v (voiced consonants)

6. Practice the difference between **speech sounds** and **vocal sounds**. Vocal sounds often have a fixed pitch, while the speech sounds usually have sliding pitch. People talk about a language melody, which shows the close relationship between song and speech. Try to slide between language melody and song.

7. Practice **high - low, strong - weak voice level**.

8. Practice the different **characters of the voice**. (Soft, breezy, excited, happy, sad, etc.)

9. Practice different ways to **amplify the tone of the vocal cords**. (main connotation - breast connotation)

10. Practice **articulation** where the throat, tongue, teeth and lips are used.

When the Church has founded a positive view of the human voice, and when it is natural to use the voice both alone and in public singing, so much is gained. (No one in the Church should feel that he cannot or may not sing in Church. Based on this positive outlook no human is "unmusical".)

Exercise 2
To discover how musical instruments work

In the psalms, man is exhorted to express his praises with everything that can give sound. (Ps. 150) It is important that the whole Church understands how musical instruments work and how they can be used. The question of how instruments should be used has always been a talking point in Christian history. The question of how musical instruments look or sound in themselves is usually not the main issue. (The allegorical interpretation of instruments that was used early in history among Christians has no sustainable biblical foundation. See Music in the kingdom of God. p 98-102)

> 1. Discover the possibilities with hands and feet. Then discover the different instrument families by confirming the family an instrument belongs to.
> 2. Play on barrels, on strings, blow into bottles and so on.
> 3. Discover the harmonic series (overtone series. In appendix 2, I show the overtone series) by means such as a birch-bark horn or a natural trumpet. (Horn or trumpet without valves.)

From the overtone series you also will find:

> 1. Intervals (distance between two tones)
> 2. Timbres, harmonies, chords (two and more tones together)
> 3. Color (timbres which we hear as different character of the tone. The same tone sounds in different instrument very different because of the color or timbre.

The overtone series has very many variations. The overtone series includes sounds and timbres that different people in the Church may feel differently about, but the Church needs to understand that God likes what he has created. That means he likes the major and minor chords, seventh chords and ninth chords. He also likes the different modes (scale systems) found in the overtone series.

When man discusses his own opinion, it is important to recognize this as human thoughts. Personal opinions not only have great influence in social communities, but also in Christian communities. It is important that the Church desires to reach a common understanding that the sounds and timbres are something God likes, even if individuals in the Church do not like some of them. Not all men like birdsong, but God does. Maybe God has some favorites among the birds, but we don't know. He hasn't spoken about this. He has valued his own creation in terms of *beautiful* and *very beautiful* (Genesis 1:25, 31) He has also declared that human voices can sing well and that skilled musicians can play well (Ezek. 33:32).

The Church cannot create in the same way as God, but it can see his majesty, beauty, and glory when it discovers and explores the sounds and rhythms in creation. The Church can be inspired by God's preaching in creation and study how God thinks and feels about sound, pulses and rhythms.

Exercise 3
Working with melodies

God has created melodies, pulses, rhythms and sounds, in a similar way that he has created the colors and shapes of animals, birds and plants. God's creativity seems to be infinitely large. There are millions of different melodies. When man makes melodies, he usually does it spontaneously, improvised or well thought out. Small children often sing while they play. The smallest children do it without the demarcation between language melody and that which has a limited scale, as it is used by adults. When adults hum or whistle melodies spontaneously, they are usually based on learned scales. Musical languages and dialects follow the same pattern of development as language development.

The exercises are designed to encourage the Church to learn the basics of how melodies are, and can be, built.

1. First whistle, hum, sing, play spontaneously (improvised) on the **basis of language melody in your own language and dialect.**
2. Whistle, hum, sing, play long and short beeps on the **same tone.** Use also rests.
3. Make melodies with **two tones.** With two tones one can make more variations.
4. Make melodies with **three and more tones.** (It isn't necessary that the melody sounds in a particular way after a traditional or a special scale.)

Exercise 4
Working with pulses and rhythms

The interval of time, which comes regularly, is called pulse or beat, for example the heart beat. The irregular interval of time is called rhythms, for example birds singing.

1. Walk with different pulses.
2. Clap your hands with different pulses.
3. Play on the instrument with different pulses.

4. Read words and sentences with different rhythms.
5. Sing and play rhythms
6. Discover also the pauses

When a Church sings rhythms together, the rhythms ought not to be too difficult. The Church should sing rhythms that work for children and untrained people. Therefore, when the Church sings together, the songs ought to be quite simple in the rhythmic structure. Rhythms that are too difficult would make many people quiet.

Exercise 5
Working with musical notation

Notation history goes back several thousand years. The exercises I propose here go from drawing lines of how a melody can move to the drawing pitches on a stave with five lines.

1. Draw a "**curve**" with high and low point. (In appendix 3 I show different examples of "curves" for the melodies.)
2. Listen how the blackbird makes and vary **short melodic motifs**. Draw short curves motifs.
3. Draw a "**skeleton**" without rhythms, for example first with curves and then with ellipses. (During the Renaissance, a style sometimes called Palestrina style, named after the composer GP Palestrina 1524-1694, was formed. When I was working with this style, I noticed that there were a lot of rules that formed the basis for building up a simple melody with whole notes. Each style has its own rules for how a melody should be formed. This makes musicians able to not only recognize different styles or the era but also to be able to point out even the composer's name.)
1. Draw **a counterpoint** to the same tune. (A melody over or under the first melody.) (See appendix 3.) Throughout history there have been different rules for how to make a counterpoint.
2. Draw different pitches as a scale on a staff and make a melody in the form AAB. Then make a melody **from a given form** such as AAB (A is a part that is repeated and B is a new part.) Use a pentatonic scale that can be formed based on an overtone series. (For example c d e g a)
3. Make melodies based on **other scales** in the overtone series.

When the Church understands of how melodies can be constructed, it can search and practice melodies out of the Jewish and Christian tradition.

Exercise 6
Working with timbre, accords or harmonies

Sounds that are together at the same times are called timbre, accord, harmonies, clang or ring and include everything from two tones to big dense clusters sounds. When the Church improvises, researches and uses harmonies, it does so usually based upon very clear subjective standpoints. The Church has been, and often is, referred to some harmonies from musical styles in history or to some fashion trend. When the Church seeks God's way in the question of which harmonic atmospheres they should nurture, it is important that they first admit the subjective feelings and standpoints held by different individuals.

In spite of these difficulties, the Church should not try to get a mishmash (farrago) from different tastes. Instead, the Church ought to ask what kind of timbres or harmonic atmospheres **best provide a space for God's Spirit to work within and through.** This position can naturally be colored by subjective interpretations. However, the attitude of seeking for an atmosphere in which God's Holy Spirit wants to be in is very important for the Church.

If the Church humbly seeks God's harmonic world, it will be led into freedom not only to improvise and research, but also to seek how the pattern of David can be and ought to be established and performed.

1. Listen to the harmonies of creation.
2. Make harmonies with different voices - be bold to try different timbres.
3. Make timbres - harmonies with instruments.

Exercise 7
Working with performing practice - interpretation

Of course God sees and hears everything that has ever happen called music. He also sees that man can perform music in many different ways. There are professional musicians who have beautiful voices and play skillfully (Ezekiel 33:32). There are those who revel around with tumultuous music under the influence of drugs. (Amos 6: 4-7; Isaiah 3: 11-12.) Beautiful voices and skillful performance (interpretation) are not enough for the Lord. It isn't enough with human ideals. Human ideals will ultimately lead to idolatry, the worship of styles or traditions, and/or to a human-centered religion. Performance practice can be justified by obviously subjective ideal pictures that have nothing to do with God. God is the Lord of the Church, who must give the Church advice about performance practice. The teaching by Jesus on this topic was to be truthful, honest, genuine and sincere. He was strongly opposed to any form of dissimulation, hypocrisy and mendacity.

1. Try different vocal sounds and different ways to express them. To practice our voices is something natural, which shouldn't be inhibited. Naturally, you want to comfort a child who screams loudly during the night hours, but Christian parents should not put a gag (muzzle) on their screaming children. Therefore, children ought to be able to practice both their voices and instruments with a lot of patience from the adult world. Nor must anyone in the Church quiet adults by saying that they are, for example, singing out of tune. In the Church, there ought to be generous opportunities for people to practice their voices and express themselves differently, provided that it is authentic, pure and from a humble heart.

2. Those who work much with their voices or/and other instruments may gradually learn performance practice. There are two basic tracks in performance practice (interpretation):

   - How a song or a piece of music was originally meant to be performed or was performed. This usually requires careful study and research.

- How it was performed in present time in different contexts. For instance, you can try to sing and play songs in different **tempos, nuances and characters.** The next phase of performing practice is about how to interpret. This means that an individual Christian and the Church express what the Holy Spirit has inspired them to. In a professional context, practice of interpretation is often done by spontaneous inspiration and learning of methods.

3. Practice various bodily ways to perform music without giving a sense of something that is inauthentic and hypocritical. Habits and manners are learned through various modes, habits and traditions. The Church, as well as individual Christians, should always be willing to analyze and examine their performance practice, their mannerisms, habits and traditions. All forms of behavior among musicians in the Church should be examined towards the character of Jesus. People listened to Jesus for what he said, but also for how he conveyed it (Mark 4:33). Jesus was genuine. But at the end of his earthly life, very few were listening to what he said, despite his narrative talent and pedagogical skills.

Exercise 8
Working with instrumentation

Instrumentation is about different ways to put instruments together. One speaks about **homogeneous and heterogeneous timbre** in the instrumentation. Homogeneous stands for combining instruments of the same family. Heterogeneous is about combining instruments from different families. One of the important elements of instrumentation is to get to know the range of an instrument and its capabilities.

4. Try adding a homogeneous orchestration of a four-part song.
5. Try adding a heterogeneous orchestration of a four-part song.
6. Vary different phrases with different instrumentation. One phrase is a part of a melody similar with a phrase in a sentence. See more at exercise 9

Exercise 9

Working with forms and structures

An important aspect of composing music is about forms and structures. It covers everything from simple sketches to finished structures. In music, there is often a thought-out form and structure, as well as in improvised music. Both improvisations and noted music have been used, and are used, in the Church. In the order (*oikonomia*), which is summarized in Christ, the source and the basic principle find expression in the audible outflow of music through beautiful forms and structures. (The same applies in art.) Musical morphology is a big subject that can be practiced from simple ditty (a simple song) forms to complex structures. At the same time, music is more than forms and structures. As previously stated, just as a stream cannot only be described as forms and structures, neither can music.

(For some in the Church this exercise maybe will be too superfluous or unnecessary.)

1. Study the forms of the songs in a hymnal.
2. Make melodies based on the following melody forms: A1 - A2 (This two-pieces form is to make a melodic phrase - A1 - and repeat the same phrase with slight changes). ABA (This three-piece melody form is to make two different phrases, and then to replay the first phrase again.)
3. Make short motifs. (This is like laying stone upon stone to form a larger building. It's about making small melodic ideas to work further with.) See the appendix

Exercise 10
Working with bodily expression

In the exercises, we have already used a lot of body expressions when we sang and played instruments. Israel was also invited to express their adoration by lifting hands, kneeling, bending their faces to the ground, jumping for joy and also dancing. The use of bodily expressions in a sexual way was altogether out of the question. The dance was about community dances and joyful, individual dances. Conducting a choir with hands is an old custom. Hand movements were used early on by the Levite leaders and the cantors in the synagogues.

1. Practice community dances.
2. Practice conducting - from simple hand signs to shape the music and inspire the Church, singers and musicians.
3. Practice expressing music with the body - both with silent and audible motions.

Exercise 11
Working with the listening culture in the Church

Listening culture in the Church gives a harvest of experiences and opinions that wields great influence over the musical life in the Church. The musical life of the Church is basically not about the tastes of individuals, families or from the Church. Rather, it's about committing yourself to building the Church out of God's thoughts and a united understanding of the Bible's teaching.

Practically, it is also about choosing songs and instrumental music that correspond to this understanding and unity (Psalm 127: 1).

Consequently, parents should talk with their children about what the Lord's will is in music; what is healthy and good to listen to. Parents are responsible for their children and for choosing songs and instrumental music, which correspond with what the Church teaches. This is an important sowing and harvest in the kingdom of God.

As I have written in my book Music in the kingdom of God I believe that Christians are not only free to sing, play and listen to old music, but also free to sing, play, listen to and compose new music in thankfulness to God. As I see it, the Church is free to explore the opportunities that sound has. However, the Church should do this out of a desire to use this opportunity in a **beautiful way, in order** and **with variety**. In practice, this means that the Church must **examine everything** and retain only that which can be used to build up the Church and give joy.

While Christians have freedom to explore musical possibilities, I believe it is the Church's duty to challenge and test the entire Western music culture based on a search for the pattern in Christ. Of course, the Western music culture isn't a universal Christian culture.

Appendix

Appendix 1

This is some examples of exercises which can be used
to practise vocal cords, throat, tongue and lips.

1   Ri   a   re   a

2   Schi   scho

3   Bo   bo   bo   bo   bo   bo

4   Skry   a   tho   a

5   Mong   a   long   a   song   a   rong   a   bong

Appendix 2

This is the harmonic series or overtone series from the tone C.
Se also https://en.wikipedia.org/wiki/Harmonic_series_(music)

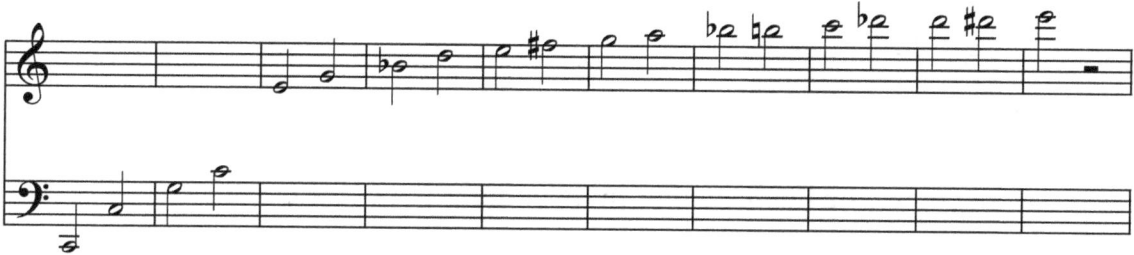

Appendix 3

This is one of the patterns for a recitative (talksinging).

Begining (initium)   middle (mediatio)   final (finalis)

Appendix 4

The curve in melodies are different.

Here is the highest point (highlight) in the beginning of the melody.

Here comes the highest point in the middle.

Here comes the highest point in the end of the melody.

Here is a stem under the melody- a so called counterpoint.

Workbook for composers and musicians

Introduction

Learning the music's material, form and its craftsmanship requires much time and effort.

This section is intended for composers and musicians who want to work more adeptly with making songs, arrangements or entire compositions for voices and instruments. In this workbook primarily it is about a few exercises to serve the Church. There are very many different titles on musical styles and musical dialects. A local Church cannot choose all kinds of music that has ever existed. Therefore, each local Church must choose the music that they want to sow and reap. Big Church groups (denominations) often choose to have a common line for which songs they want to sing and what kind of music they want to use. They make their own hymnbooks, and sometimes their own publication of sheet music.

It is not possible for Christian composers and musicians to learn thousands of styles. Each composer and musician has to choose one or a few style areas with which he/she wants to work. Concerning sing able melodies for singing in the Church, a musician can take a basic position to search in the entire treasury of songs that has ever existed within Christianity. If one analyzed this treasury of songs only, it would still leave a lot of choice for the local Church. This means that when someone doing their own melodies, arrangements or compositions, they need to decide upon one or a few styles and some forms.

For Christianity as a whole, there ought to be a common understanding of how the pattern of David was continued and how it can continue today. Therefore, the Church today may ask where the pattern from David developed – how it was passed down in the first century.

When the Church is willing to deal with the replacement culture – which early took place - there is also an opportunity to talk about and practicing a common Christian music culture. Without this common restoration of David's pattern it is a naive utopia to talk of a common Christian music culture. Probably the Church may wait until Jesus comes back before this heavenly music culture becomes a reality on earth.

Some basic reflections based on the order in the overtone series

As I am now doing a deeper study of the overtone series, I do it with the desire to see the beautiful order that is revealed in creation. It isn't an attempt to present my own views about what is beautiful or ugly, but rather simply to try to describe the beauty of God's order.

The overtone series has a so-called major chord as a fundament. It means that this constellation of tones is beautiful as God's order of creation. This major chord is then coloured with a minor seventh and a major ninth. In these over tones, you can also find the so-called minor chord. The minor cords can also be coloured with a major sixth. So major - minor and colourings are the fundament in the overtone series.

Reflection 1

The minor second, the major seventh and the minor none are not prominent colour of the chords in the overtone series. When one uses this interval in the chords, the chords can look like spices. God has created both colours and tones, spices and many other things that has been used in different ways.

Reflection 2

Major and minor chords in the overtone series are prominent. To have these as the fundament of composing is, therefore, natural. Starting with the overtone series in composition or musicianship is neither a force, a necessity, a Christian doctrine nor something universal.

All tones in the major and minor chords are doubling in the overtone series.

Reflection 3

When you go from one tone to another in a melody, a **parallel flowing of the stems (parts)** arises in fact. It is chords or harmonies that move in parallel. When proposing rules for how the stems may flow, it is called rules for **polyphony** (voice leading rules). Such a rule could be that every stem should move independently, specifically not too unison parallel. Such rules are common in Western music. This is a human way to do it. That doesn't mean it's necessarily bad, but it is required for the Church to recognize that there are subjective values.

Reflection 4

When writing four or more stems there are many ways to work. If the glory from Jesus' face could been painted or expressed in music, the pattern would have been quite easy to reconstruct and handed over. But the pattern from David is not described in the Bible as an icon, that could be used to determine which voice leading rules the music in the Church should follow. Rather, the apostle Peter told about a relationship with Jesus Christ and an atmosphere of faith, love, indescribable heavenly joy and jubilation (1 Pet. 1: 8).

Therefore, it is impossible to give clear rules for the stems which the music in the Church ought to have. When one becomes marked by and inspired through a relationship with Jesus, there will be fruit in how a composer and musician form a harmonic atmosphere in and around himself and the Church.

As I have written in Music of the kingdom of God (p.141-142) there is a risk in making mathematically correct music icons. Then the chord and voice leading rules become a regulatory system to live up to rather than a person to live with and follow. That said, there is obviously still a freedom to "paint" the beautiful art of tones based on rules, forms and craftsmanship, provided it does not became my god whom I live for. For many of the so-called classical composers and musicians, there was not a contradiction between craftsmanship and a deep and warm relationship to Jesus. Playful, spontaneous music (improvisation) could and can also be an expression of a warm relationship with Jesus.

I propose, therefore, in this reflection that you examine the tonal possibilities based in the overtone series and then choose which sound atmosphere you want to express.

As I understand, Christians are free to explore possibilities in harmonies and chords based on the overtone series and then select which ringing atmosphere they want to express. When one leaves the overtone series and major and minor thinking and explores cluster sounds, is it important to see and listen to how God has created harmonies in creation. Composers and musicians cannot create a babbling brook, but nevertheless they can be inspired by the beauty of creation. But, remember, it is the relationship with Jesus Christ, the very source of inspiration for Christian composers and musicians, that music inspired of God will flow.

Exercises

You are permitted to make copies of this part
but not in a commercially purpose.

Exercises - melodies

The first exercise is about discovering the range (ambitus) for a melody that the church will sing. The lowest notes should not be lower than **a** in the small octave and the maximum should not be higher than **e²**. (See 1)

1. Start by doing "**sketches**", first with "**curves**". (See 2)
2. Then work with small **motifs.** Use both curves and notes. (See 3)

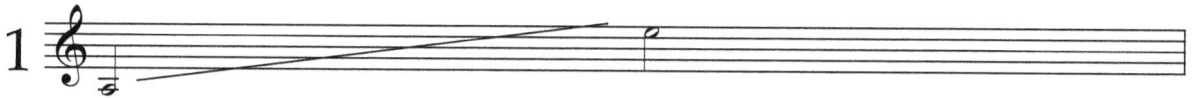

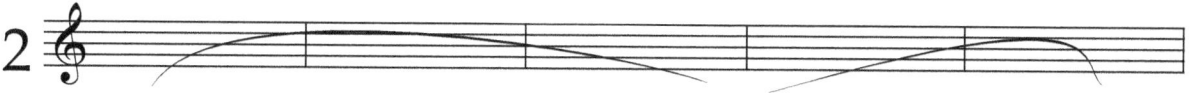

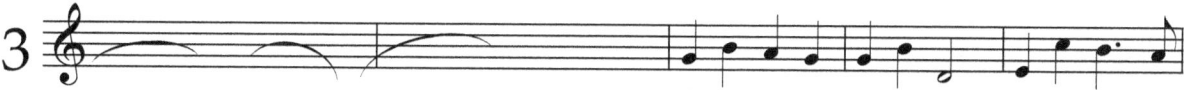

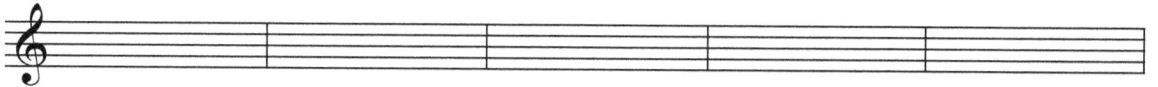

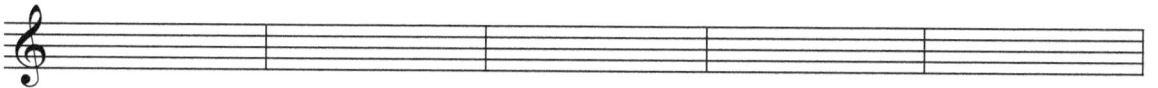

Exercises - rhythms

Add rhythms to the "sketches".
Improvise and test with many varieties of rhythms. (See 4)

Exercises - phrases and forms

When making a melody it is like creating different phrases (sentences) in a text.
These phrases can be very different. Often one uses different **forms.**
The form theory of melodies is about how melodies are built.

A melody consists of **intervals** forming small **motifs.**
These motifs then form **phrases** and phrases form a **melody.**

If you make several phrases without any repetition you can call this form
one piece (A).
If you make two similar phrases this could be called **two piece** melody **(A1 A2).**
A melody can be made with two different phrases (AB), the first of which is
repeated after the B phrases **(ABA)** called **three piece** melody.
The melody form is called **barform (AAB)**
when the first part is repeated before the B phrase.

Make melodies for the following forms:

A - onephrase

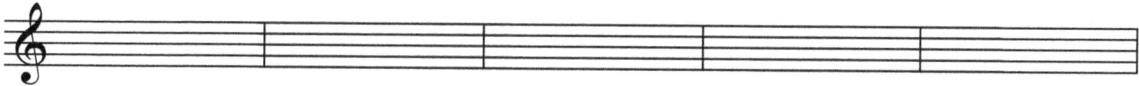

A A - twophrase

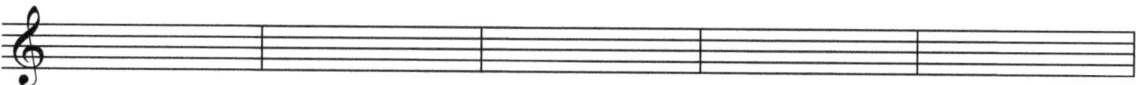

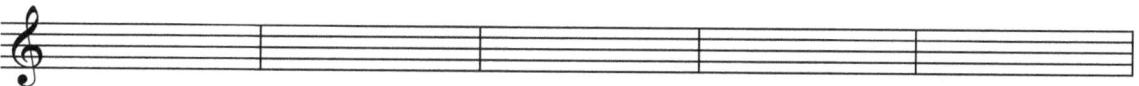

A B A - two phrases in threepart

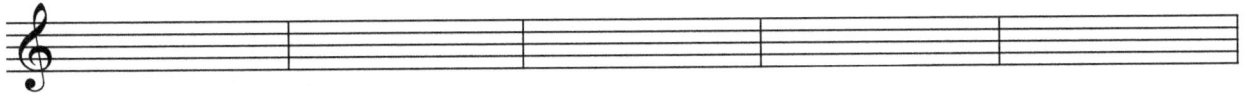

A A B - Barform

A A B A - two phrases in threepart

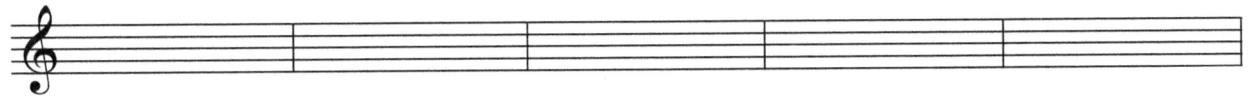

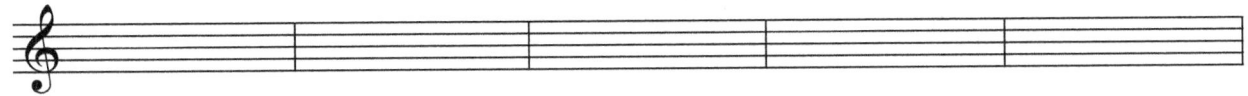

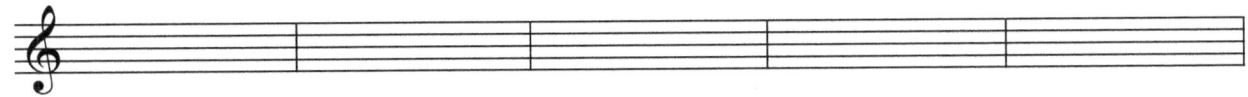

Exercises - texts

Words have one or more **syllables.**

Words are emphasized differently. (For example morning __ _ Stavanger_ __ _)

If you have more notes on one syllable it is called **melisma.**

A text can be read with a permanent beat on each syllable.

You can also make rhythms to the text (as you usually read texts).

1. Makes rhythms to a text from the Bible.

   Make the first based on speech and language rhythm.

2. Then do the same exercise with a pulse.

3. Write down the rhythms and then make melody to the text.

   Texts often have different meter classes. This means that you count all

   the syllables in a phrase. Syllables in an entire melody can

   for example be 8 + 6 + 8 + 6 + 8 + 8. (Each phrase is counted separately.)

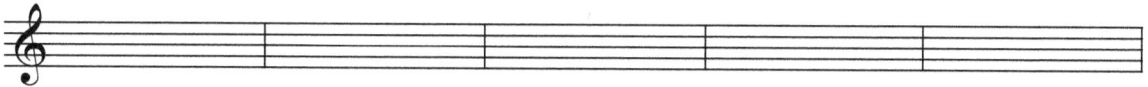

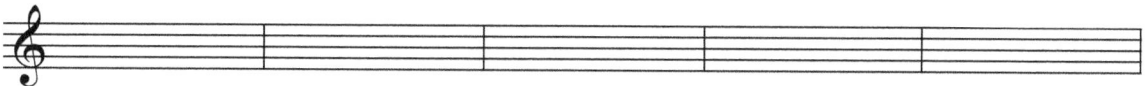

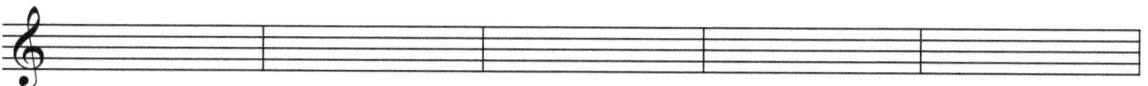

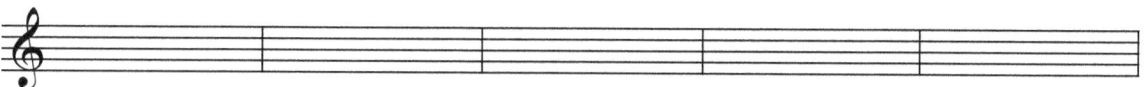

Exercises - parts

Make two, three and four-part exercises based on the two different ways
of working with parts (stems):

1. Horizontal - add stem on another. Make the first freely without
   any special rules. Continue writing in different styles.
   (Working Exercises for different styles can be found
   in various books and also online, for example,
   http://kmh.diva-portal.org/smash/get/diva2:694372/FULLTEXT01.pdf)

2. Vertical - put two, three and four melodies alongside one another.
   Make the first freely without rules. Continue typing the basis of rules
   in different styles. (See voicing rules in different styles based on other books.)

Here are some basic concepts of how the stems can move together.

One stem moves, the other moves not.

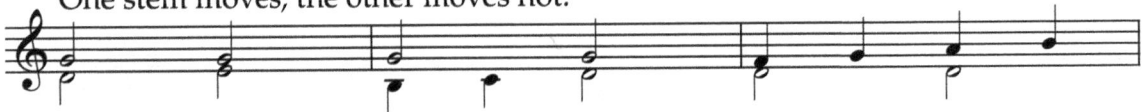

The stem moves contra each other.

The stem moves together in the same direction.

The stem moves with the same interval.

Exercises - clangs

In the exercise of writing stems we have already
formed a clang with two tones.
If you write more stems there will be clangs with three, four, five tones.
Examine many different kinds of clangs to a melody.

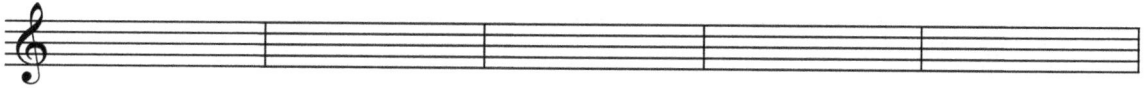

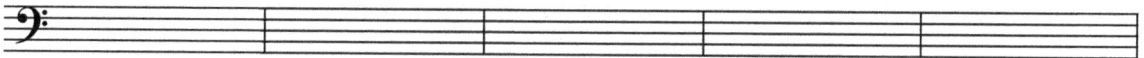

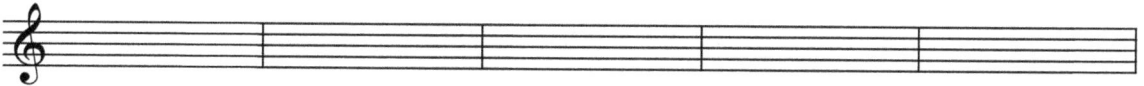

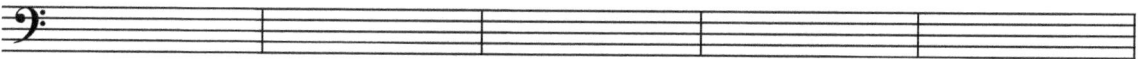

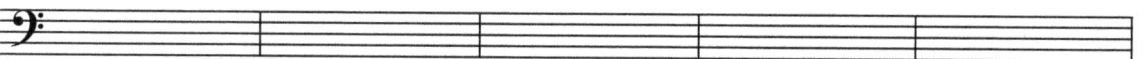

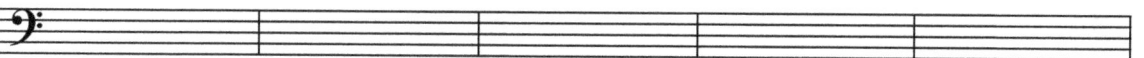

Exercises - instrumentation

The first you need to learn concerning using instruments
is to get acquainted with the instrument's **timbre** and **range (ambitus).**
It is also important to find out where in the range it is best to play.
Read about this and then write some four part songs for the following instruments:
Flute, oboe, saxophone, French horn, trumpet, violin, cello, bass
Then try different combinations of instruments.

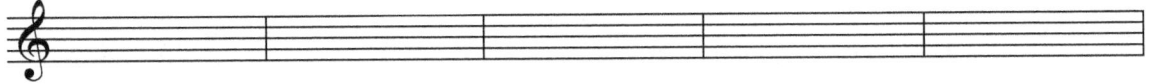

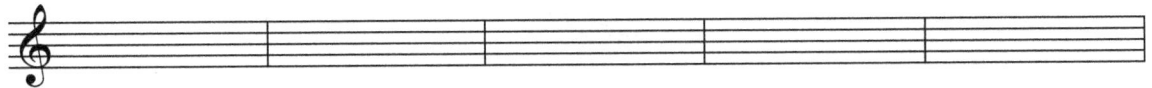

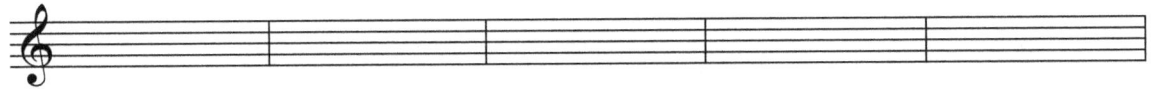

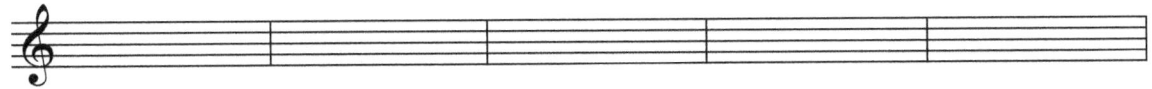

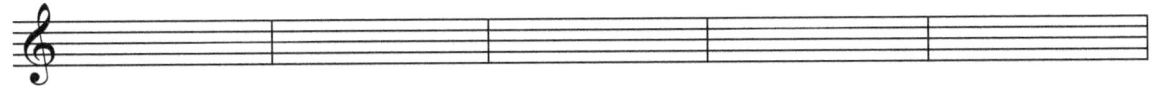

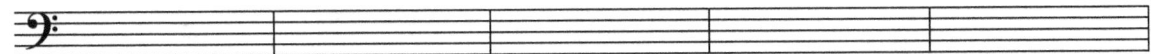

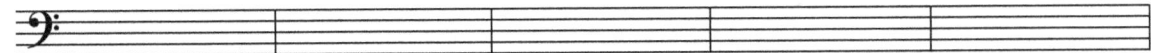

Exercises - structure

Composed music is often structured with three main layers.
(Study example Bach's Inventions, sinfonier and Wohltemperierters Klavier.)

1. rhythmic idea (Make a rhythmic idea above the staves.)
2. melodic idea (Make a melody for cello on the rhythmic idea.)
3. contrapuntal idea - an idea of how one or more stems can be formed together.
   (Make a stem over the melody as a contrast to the melody.)

Study structures and order in creation.
There are all types of structures from simple to very complex rhythmic structures.
The melodies, signals, and the sounds are from one or two tones and
to highly complex and diverse motives operations.
The clang structure is very complex and varied.

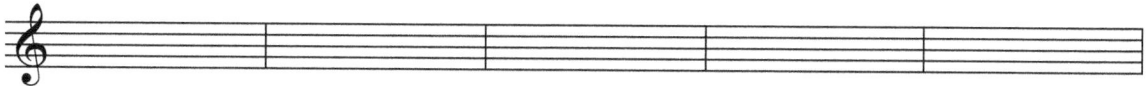

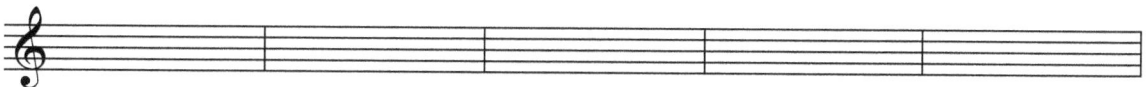

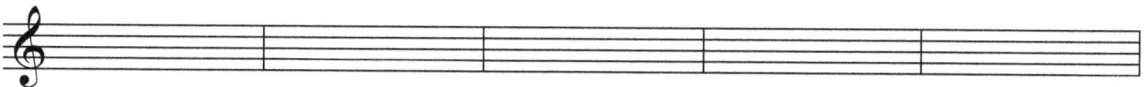

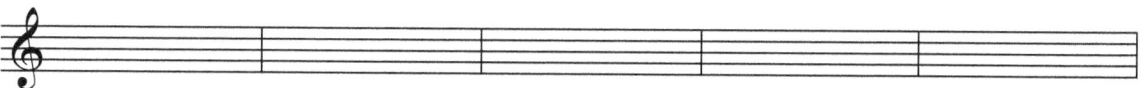

Exercises - performing practise

A melody or a whole piece of music can be performed in many different ways.
The **perfoming pratice (interpretation)** has two main parts:

1. To give detailed instructions as to how **phrasing, tempo, nuance** and **character**
   in the melody or a piece of music should be. (In European music from
   the Middle Ages up to midst of 18th century the composers didn't
   write out detailed instructions. It is necessary then to research how voices
   and musical instruments sounded, how they played and how performances
   could have been. People also want to perform the music in as authentic
   a manner as possible.)

2. to allow contemporary musicians to decide upon the execution.
   Propose phrasing tempo, nuance and character on a melody you write.

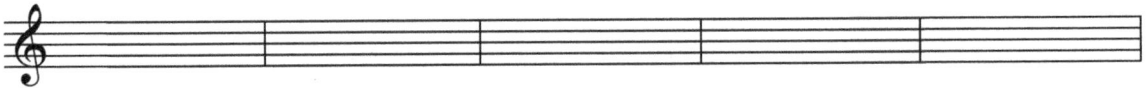

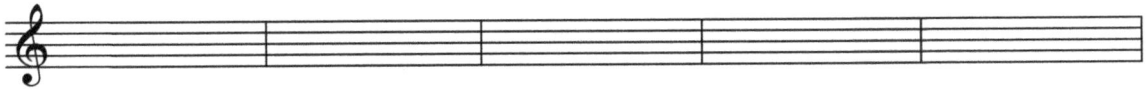

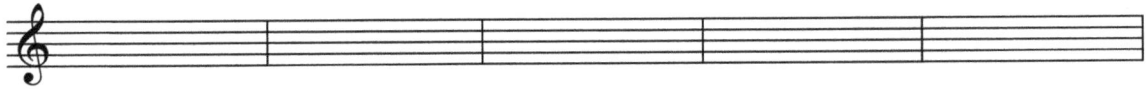

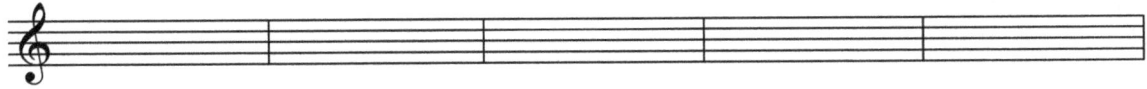

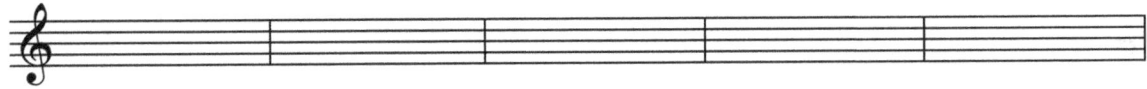

Exercises - tonality and atonality

It is often said that **tonality** is a special organization of tones, eg, a scale
with a tonal center. Within this oganisation of tones the melody circuits,
but can be extended with modulations, with so-called character tones that lead
the melody toward to another tonality.

From tonality can one use modulations to dissolve tonality and
the sense of a tonal center and go further on to so-called **atonality.**

1. Practice making melodies in different tonality.
2. Practice using the character tones and make modulations in the melody.
3. Practice making atonal melodies.

The end of the phrase in a melody are called **cadence.**
The word cadence is mostly used for different chord passages in the end of
the phrase .
4. Read about cadences and make different cadences, both with
and without chord settings.

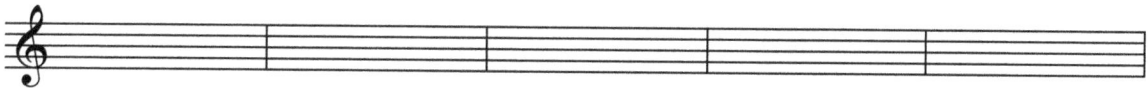

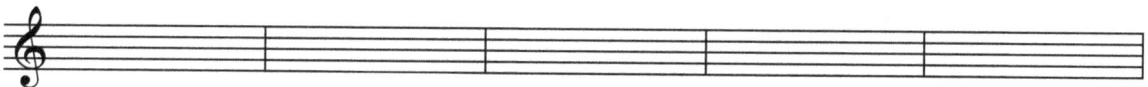

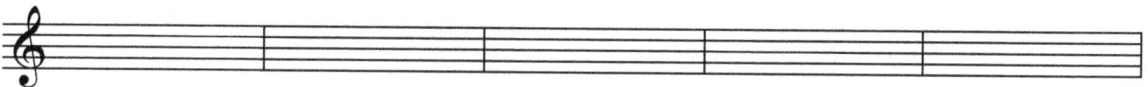

The pattern from David – a summary with Bible passages

- The beginning of the Levite service is described in Deuteronomy 10: 8. They were *separated ...to stand before the Lord to minister to Him and to bless in His name, to this day.* Compare with Psalm 81:1-6.

- Then later David received a pattern from the hand of the Lord. It came through the Spirit. The Lord had commanded this through His prophets. It was a royal decree.

- 1 Chron. 28: 11-19; 2 Chron. 29:25; Neh. 11:23

- There was a definite order day by day. They ministered morning and evening. 1 Chronicles 23:30

- 288 which were particularly educated. They were skilled. They had wisdom from God and were both willing and skilled. 1 Chronicles 25: 7-8; 28:21; 30: 21-22; Ps 47: 8 (Hebrew *sachel* wise, skilled)

- 4000 served as musicians at the time of David.

- The training took place as a prentice system. The knowledgeable (skilled) and the disciples were together. 1 Chronicles 25: 8

- They sang sometimes antiphonal. Neh. 12:24 Comp. Eph. 5:19

- The leaders took up the praise songs. Neh. 11:17

- They had prophetic spirit. 1 Chronicles 25: 2-3

- They had blow, string and percussion instruments, ie all kinds of instruments. 1 Chronicles 15:42; 25: 1

www.ingramcontent.com/pod-product-compliance
Lightning Source LLC
Chambersburg PA
CBHW080531030426
42337CB00023B/4694